'I Never Feel Old'

Frances Caldwell Durland

'I Never Feel Old'

An 88-year-old shares her positive approach to the challenges of aging

Cover, book design and illustrations by Julie Van Leeuwen.

SBN 0-912228-78-4

Dedication

To all who love the gift of life
and express its joy.
They never really grow old;
the years add only grace
and a sense of God's wonder.

Foreword

What does it mean to be old? To Frances Caldwell Durland, it has little to do with the 88 years she has accumulated. To her, "old" is an attitude, a sad conviction that life has grown dull and drab and uninteresting.

By that standard, Mrs. Durland is very young.

Maintaining a youthful spirit is a matter of choice, according to this lady. She does not pretend the choice is always easily made; she freely admits the stress and anxiety that can accompany aging. She has herself known the pain of sudden widowhood, limitations imposed by illness, the distress of failing eyesight. Through it all, however, she has remained warm, sympathetic and filled with enthusiasm.

To her contemporaries Mrs. Durland offers the personal insights, practical suggestions and inspirational beliefs that keep her life exciting. And to those whose years are yet an unimpressive tally, she lends understanding of both the rewards and the struggles of a long life.

The editors
Saint Anthony Messenger Press

Contents

Chapter 1

Reflections of a Reluctant Old Lady

A few months ago I spent a rare day across the bay in San Francisco. Overhead a few fluffy bits of leftover fog draped the highest buildings. The sea was a deep blue-green. Alcatraz, shining in the sun, guarded the gate to the open sea.

As I gazed at the view I thought, "How beautiful! Life is such a gift. I don't ever want to lose this feeling of joy and wonder."

At the end of the day, I stood on the crowded platform waiting for the commuter train to take me back across the bay. As the train glided into the station, I heard a voice behind me say, "Let the old lady on first."

I looked around to see where the old lady was. I couldn't see her. "Oh dear," I realized, "*I* am the old lady."

I flounced onto the train. Not for a minute was I grateful for the strangers' good manners. "Old lady, indeed!" I sniffed. I *never* feel old. I am full of the juice of life. Once in a while my body signals that all is not as youthful as it once was, but I ignore it.

As the train glided into the underwater tunnel, I remembered my birthday party a short time before. Such a charming party it was, with a cake and candles and all the trimmings. The conversation turned to old ladies who in their 80's were having such a time, poor dears.

To this moment my age had been a carefully guarded secret. Like Jack Benny, I was a perennial 39. Abruptly, I was weary of the talk about poor old ladies. In my sweetest manner I announced, "I am 87 today."

The results were all I could have desired: "Impossible!" "No one would ever know!"

So as the train pulled out of the underwater tunnel, I felt a grin starting down inside me. "Oh well," I thought, "I don't have to *feel* old."

Still, this seems to be the year comments on age pursue me. My daughter and I recently took a trip to Hawaii. One morning as she swam in an impossibly blue sea, I sat on a chair and gazed at the scene. I was very conscious of the beauty of the world, of palm trees waving to the sky, of white sand listening to the constant lap of the incoming sea. Out near the horizon the white clouds swung through the sky.

My thoughts were very much on the wonder of God's gifts. I felt a sense of being part of this wonder. A deep peace and contentment filled me—until my mood was interrupted by an elderly man.

He sat down in a nearby chair, facing me. I was somewhat surprised, but the unexpected has a magnetic attraction for me. What was going to happen?

"Good morning." He looked out to sea, then back to me. "How old are you?"

Probably I gasped. It seemed a bit unusual. But since keeping flexible is part of my reluctance to age, I pulled myself together. I did not exactly answer, just hinted that I was not youthful.

"About my mother's age," the stranger announced. "You had an easy life?"

There was not time to review my life in detail, but hurriedly I decided it had not been too hard. He nodded.

"You don't look old," he noted with gravity.

Our conversation quickly languished, since we did not seem to have much in common beyond curiosity. Discouraged at the lack of communication, he left me—thinking about my age.

I have an unending curiosity about why this happens and that, about what makes me tick, or you, or whoever. I think that the very trait of unceasingly asking why, why, *why* tends to longevity. It keeps me alive and in the stream of life. If my age is a topic of such great interest to others, perhaps I had better probe and see what I come up with as a philosophy.

3

To begin with, I feel that life is a gift, a beautiful gift from God. I think that we are meant to live as fully and abundantly as we can, seeking always to grow in the spirit, accepting whatever comes with praise and courage. To me, there is no such thing as "old" unless I myself choose to become old, because my spirit is eternal.

I am willing to grant that aging is not always an easy road. Sometimes it is a very lonely one. But it is one of the cycles of life. I feel with my whole being that I can make it a very beautiful one if I have an indomitable spirit. After all, I have been going through various cycles since birth. This, in some ways, is the final challenge.

By an indomitable spirit I mean being flexible, for one thing. I can take anything that comes—not by setting my jaw and grimly enduring, but by opening my heart and letting God fill it with love and faith. Thus he gives the inward strength to meet whatever challenges come: physical, emotional or spiritual.

No two of us will meet the same challenges, for each of us is as unique as the snowflakes which fall to the ground. It has not been easy for me to accept many of the problems which have come. But I have met other challenges all along the road—conquered some, failed at others. I can manage now.

It is important to believe that I can. Somehow a myth has grown up that the old should retire from life (with grace) at a suitable age. I am very reluctant to do any such thing. I believe we are given life to live as richly and fully as possible *at all ages*.

4

The myth saps self-confidence. It's difficult to believe in myself when I am constantly told I am not up to snuff, or treated as if I am suddenly unable to make decisions. I rebel at the idea that just because I am now 88 my mind is too foggy to function. Nonsense!

I am having the joyous experience of being more myself than ever before, and reveling in it. I am I! That inner core of me, God's child, is no different now than in past years. When I get discouraged and decide life is a luxury I can't afford any longer, I remember all the pain, sorrow and joy I have experienced. Thank you, God. I have lived—really lived.

We have to choose the kind of old age we want. I prayed. I decided that I would live fully, open myself to life as long as I can breathe. The qualities which enriched life at 20 or 50 are the ones that create a vital, vivid, joyful old age.

I am sure life is meant to be profound, real and deep. I make decisions, but no longer without listening to the guidance of the Holy Spirit within. Sometimes I make mistakes or think my wishes are God's words, but I learn. I have the feeling that adventure is just around the corner—and I keep rushing toward it. I simply do not have time to think about being old. I am indeed, a reluctant old lady, if "old" means shutting myself off from life.

Some people sing a constant refrain: "I am too old to do this or that, to go here or there." But I plan to be on the go as long as I can stand up and walk (with my trusty cane).

Of course I attempt to use common sense. And each decade beyond 50 has certainly depleted physical energy. However, my body is only a part of me. It may be very uncomfortable; yet "me," that real person inside, feels just fine. No experience is ever wasted; now while there's still time is the time to have fun.

A friend in her 60's confessed, under pressure, to being a frustrated actress. She joined a little theater group as wardrobe mistress, using her ability to sew. Finally she was given a small part. She soared on wings of creativity—while her family sighed, "Oh, Mother, at your age!"

At first, she says, she felt foolish. Then pride came to life. "I'm glad I did it!" she almost shouted. "It keeps me young. Don't forget you too will grow old."

Not all of us share my friend's ambition, but whatever urge to try something new stirs, I am all for fulfilling it. It is exciting to find unsuspected potential hidden away inside oneself. It keeps me so keyed up about life itself I forget all about how old I am supposed to be.

It is an accepted fact that chronological age really is not true age. I know some 25-year-olds who already have all the earmarks of "old age." What then is "old"? It is when life gets to be dull, drab, uninteresting because we have ceased to be a vital part of it.

The more intensely we live in the *now*, experiencing life in every moment, hour, day, the more vibrant and alive the later years will be. We

6

don't have to say no to life. We can sing out a loud firm, "Yes, life, I love you! I fling myself right into your fast-moving stream."

Someone said to me, "Life has become a long, dark and lonely tunnel for me. I am too old." She sighed. "I feel alone and frightened, calling for help which never comes."

That is sad. There have been days in my life when I too felt frightened and alone. They were by no means all in my later years. As a child or a young adult, I found rejection was so painful I sometimes inhibited impulses to offer myself. I no longer allow myself that liberty.

In maturity, surely some lessons of faith have been learned. One such lesson is that through pain and suffering comes compassion. There is no promise in the Bible that I will never know pain; how could I grow if I never met a challenge? "I am with you always" (Matthew 28:20) is the promise which has comforted me again and again.

As more and more years are added to my life, I feel more certain that living does not mean only to experience pleasure. It is a constant growth toward wholeness. I am responsible for that growth, no one else. At every cycle of life, new lessons had to be learned. I had to rise above the anguish and pains of life to turn whatever experience came into victory.

I am glad for all the lessons on the meaning of life and myself in it and my relationship to God. I am so grateful for the flow of God's life within me.

Life—we use the word so lightly. Yet life is not just a word; it is that which makes us move and have

7

our being. It is the flow of God's love and energy in our body, mind and soul. It is a gift beyond words. I feel such wonder, such gratitude at being given so many years.

I want to have the judgment to take care of my body, but not to be ruled by it. I want to keep my mind alive by enriching it with great books rather than listening to negative reports. I do not want to separate myself from the sorrows of the world. Last but by no means least, I want to serve in whatever way seems given to me, for in so doing, I also serve Christ.

I do not expect to feel or conduct myself as I did when young. I love the word *dignity* and hope to have it without sacrificing humor or warmth of manner. I think of these last years as the culmination of all life has offered me: love, joy, pain, suffering, light-heartedness at the right moments.

Wonderful things still happen: unexpected beauty, love beyond what I deserve. My prayer is, "Let me be responsive, Lord. Let me be an instrument for you." I am sure that God never thinks of me as old.

Every morning on awakening, my first thought is that I am glad to be alive. I wonder what will happen this day. Will I meet some new and exciting person, or have an emotional experience that enriches my life?

The minute I stop feeling like that I will know I am getting old. I fervently hope I will never join the people who sit twiddling their thumbs, so to speak, because life is dull and they are bored. How can I be bored? If I am, I can at least change the furniture around or stir up my imagination.

"But I am old and frail," some protest. Sometimes that is true. But we do not lose our self-esteem just because we are ill. Courage is a form of faith, I find, and the Comforter waits for our call.

I would become old if I let my imagination die. Then the world would be dull, colorless. What joy to let my mind and heart go leaping and dancing! I want to see the world with eyes of love and joy, not with criticism and bitterness—for that is "old."

I don't want to be like a dried-up leaf on an old tree, a leaf which finally falls silently to the ground. I want to vibrate with all the excitement and joy of whatever is around me, visible and invisible. Then I know that I am alive, whether a reluctant old lady or a person who has opened wide her spirit to the mighty love and power of God.

Chapter 2

Discovering Values

When I was given the opportunity recently to speak before a group of people interested in learning more about the problems of age, I found a genuine thrill.

While visiting my daughter, I met a young man from Washington, D.C., who is deeply involved in working with elderly people. He invited me to share with him a workshop for people who had an elderly person in the home or who were training to become helpers in institutions. I felt a little scared, because I have never considered myself a speaker. But I also felt that maybe, just maybe, I had something helpful to offer.

Facing that large group of people and trying to share my own experiences was a new step in discovering values. First, I became aware again how wonderful and responsive people are. I felt I was the recipient, not the people to whom I spoke.

Another gain was the renewed realization that elderly people deeply need reassurance of their own value, their right to feel proud. I felt that need myself and found it to some extent fulfilled by the sharing of that group as we discussed some of the points brought up.

And I discovered a value I had not been aware of before. I did not know that I could stand up in front of a group of strangers and feel that they were all friends, that we shared a real and beautiful search for understanding. It was a very humbling experience.

One of the comments made by a person in the group gave me a new insight and set me thinking about values: "Not everyone has had your opportunities for education. How do you feel about others' reactions to growing old?"

Life has given me some opportunities not everyone has had. On the other hand, some have had far more. As I thought about it, it seemed to me our values are a question of character rather than formal education. Life is an excellent teacher, if we are open to it. Some of the most spiritually mature people I know have had few cultural or educational opportunities. Somehow they had formed values which made them grow.

Isn't the capacity to discover new values as life

teaches us an expression of growing wholeness? Practical values certainly change as one ages. The rush and hurry of earlier days gives way to more leisure. Building a career or guiding and nurturing a family through the early years is a struggle which ends. This is the point where many people flounder, trying to find purpose and reality in life.

I have been very fortunate in that my interests and hobbies are such that age need not hamper them. But I confess to considerable irritation at my inability to keep at something as long as I once did. And in that problem I find a new value, a virtue I have long needed: patience. I have had to learn to be content with doing one hour of work instead of three or four at a stretch.

In the process, I have learned to understand others whose physical strength has never been equal to the demands of life. This understanding brings me to the realization that my values have deepened in spirituality. Material things are far less important; human relationships are far more valuable.

In warm and wonderful relationships I have found the greatest values. Life is not beautiful because of the things around me, although nature plays a great part in my sense of the vitality of all life. The beauty lies, rather, in growing awareness of the sheer wonder of the human soul. More and more I see Christ in each person, whether attractive or seemingly unlovable.

Another question put to me in the discussion with that group was, "If you could live your life over, would you change any of it?" I would, for instance, raise my children differently. But I no longer wish it could have been different, that I could have had this or done that. I feel very strongly that while there are parts of my life I may always regret, on the whole I am sure God gave me every experience to help me grow.

I think it is necessary to look on our mistakes as part of the growth plan. No one grows on a diet of complete ease in all areas of life. I do not regret any of the pain or suffering, for in overcoming it I learned compassion and forgiveness—toward others and toward myself.

More recently I spoke before a group of nurses who work with the elderly ill. Illness, of course, is one of the saddest parts of being old. The body does wear out; brain damage occurs. I have no right to say anything on this matter for, as one of the nurses said, "You must have excellent health. You appear well."

It is true that, compared with many my age, I have good health even though I feel the limitations. The miracle of my well-being is a never-ending source of praise and thanks to God. I believe that as my own feeling about the reality of the living Christ has deepened, my health has improved.

I have had TB, a cancer operation and many other serious illnesses. Every time, I have turned to the healing flow of God's love and felt that, as I accepted the energy of that love, my well-being improved.

Twelve years ago I began having severe angina attacks. Some two or three years later, my doctor said, "I think we have this stabilized. You should have two or three years of reasonable activity!"

Not for a moment am I implying that whatever improvement has occurred since then is due to any power in me. On the contrary, it can only be a reflection of my own growing understanding of the Spirit's power combined with the medicine I take.

I believe, however, with my whole heart and soul that any of us can deter physical waning in our later years by a profound belief that God's life is in us as long as we live. I do not mean that illness strikes people who have failed to be Christian. But when God is a close reality, some universal and cosmic energy flows into us.

Another of the nurses asked me, "How do you get an elderly patient to want to help herself? I have a patient who will do nothing for herself, even though she could. It would help her health—and me, too—if she would try."

I did not feel I had the wisdom to answer her question. But my feeling is that such a person has lost all self-respect and desperately needs to feel loved. Resignation is never the answer. We have all lived; we all have something to offer. Service to others—whatever our ability and opportunity—is a lifeline.

In honesty, I have at times heartily resented having to grow spiritually. It is much easier to think old age is too hard, to relax and take up some harmless hobby which bores one stiff but is not demanding.

I have always loved to dance—especially folk

and square dancing. I am very envious of those who can still dance in their lively old age. Unfortunately, it is my lot to be a very reluctant onlooker.

I had to learn that there is a time and a place for all things, and that fuming and fussing because I can no longer be that active is not growth. Instead I must find another form of self-expression—listening to music, reading, painting. Even my reading is now being denied me by failing eyesight. So how am I going to retain the sense of joy and wonder in life?

The greatest value of all, I have learned, is to let go and let God manage my life. Daily periods of silent contemplation and meditation, coupled with reading the Bible and other inspirational works, has made genuinely joyful old age possible.

God gave me this life and with it the choice of what to think and say, do and feel. He has given me all the gifts to create a world of joy. That joy has nothing to do with what is happening to me; it is the knowledge that I am his beloved child.

Nothing is lost, nothing I have ever enjoyed. It is all in my inner being, in memory, in experience. It is all part of me forever, and that is what makes life real and glorious.

I am willing to accept that there are cycles in life. Part of the spiritual maturity which I seek is being able to accept changes with serene confidence that other joys will take the place of old loves. I want to live—fully, completely—and fill out all the empty spaces in that person who is "me" from birth to death.

Chapter 3

Friendship

"All my old and real friends are either dead or moved far away," lamented a woman I know. "I am very lonely."

I am sorry for her. But I do not believe there is ever a time when we cannot make friends. I am not quite sure why so many people, as they reach 70 or 80, feel hesitant about reaching out to make new friends. Perhaps it is the lack of confidence instilled in us by the myth that the old are somehow different from the young. This, of course, is nonsense. Our deepest feelings and desires are the same ones we had years ago. The need for closeness is as much a reality as ever.

Our family and our friends are our links with life. To be stable and secure it is essential to have these warm relationships. The person who withdraws from life creates a vacuum around himself or herself.

All our lives our friends have shared with us the place where we were in our development. In these later years, I find new friends who answer the needs, emotional or otherwise, of my present state of being. Some of the most wonderful friends I have ever had I have found in the past 10 years. Many are younger than I am—10, 30, even 80 years younger—but that has nothing to do with the quality of friendship.

I value people more than I did in my early years. They are gifts to me; I have a deep reverence for friendship. Friendship holds comfort and wonder— and sometimes pain. It involves trust and mystery, the mystery of coming to know and understand another. I need to keep in touch with the feelings and desires, joys and sorrows of others to be truly alive.

And, presumably, I am better equipped to be a friend. I am mature (I hope!) and have lived enough to be able to put self aside and enter into the needs of my friend. I do not expect perfection from my friends anymore. Nor do I want to bind them to me in any way. Life has taught me the beauty of freedom and how to love without demanding.

The wonder of friendships is how varied they are. No two persons are alike; no two friends proffer the same qualities. Hence my response and theirs is different in each relationship. While not everyone appeals to me as a friend, I am profoundly aware that to open myself to friendship among those quite different from myself in age, ideas and background means that I am enriching my own life.

My friendship with the very young, especially with my youngest grandchild who lives nearer than the rest, stimulates my imagination. He lives, part of the time, in the same world I do. He also lives in another world, one he has created around himself, in which he sees and responds to many things which I have almost forgotten. He is bursting with love and energy and the joy of life; he renews in me the conviction that I must revitalize my own responses to life. His love flows out of him, reminding me that I need not hoard mine.

I find joy in all contacts with the young because they see life freshly, and I see again with them. They remind me that everything is a gift from God and must be accepted with grace. They remind me that only by keeping my own mind and heart in tune with the wonder of the world can I possibly stay young in spirit.

Some new friends I found close at hand: my children. The transition from parent to friend is a whole new adventure.

It is sometimes difficult for me to realize that my children are middle-aged and quite capable of running their own lives without interference from me. This change has presumably been going on for years, but now and then I become overly impressed with my own wisdom and have to back off to start over again with a son or daughter.

Friendship with my middle-aged children has

been very important to my efforts to remain youthful in heart and mind. I find their points of view in this changing world stimulating, sometimes exasperating, but never boring.

I am aware that being old is one thing in their minds, another in mine. They are considerate and careful not to imply they think I have lost my ability to function on my own. But in moments of feeling my age (strictly in my body, you understand), I wish that for five minutes they could *know* how it feels to have to be careful about this and that. For no one at 88 escapes moments of feeling as if one is falling apart.

When I was young I was always told that making friends was not difficult if I was friendly myself. I have found this equally true as an old lady—reluctantly old, you remember. Instead of wondering if I am going to be acceptable to a new group or a new person, I follow the suggestions given so many years ago: Be warm, friendly, interested in the other person. It works like a charm.

I believe the only person who has a problem making new friends in old age is one who has forgotten other people are also lonely. Riding the public bus one day, I sat next to a woman who suddenly started telling me her life story. Why this happened, I am not sure. My feeling is that she simply needed to talk to someone who was willing to listen and not condemn—for it was a strange story she told, one that held evil and disillusionment. The episode brought home to me how lonely some people are. Our friendship only lasted the length of the ride, but each of us took something important away.

Traveling is an excellent way to find new friends. Church activity is another. And there are few towns which do not have a very active senior citizens' group.

When I was young, I would never have dreamed of going up to someone in a group who looked interesting to me and introducing myself. Now I would not hesitate. I am too afraid of missing something exciting and vital. It is possible I will be rejected. That may hurt for a moment, but it will not really be important as it was when I was young. Normality is a necessity only to youth—and to the old who have lost their enthusiasm for life.

This spontaneity has nothing to do with losing dignity. Dignity is an expression of integrity within and is protective.

Not long ago I attended a singles' meeting with a friend. There I did not get the feeling of genuine and active pleasure. Later, as a guest who had recently published a book on grief, I was asked to speak.

As I spoke, I had the feeling of a deep, hidden need in the group. I felt compassion, for I know that same sense of loneliness, the hunger and thirst for meaningful relationships. I believe all of us need to be sensitive to this hidden loneliness. A friend is one who shares this unspoken loneliness—and without friends, the last years may be very dull and drab.

Entertaining is one way in which I handle my own need for companionship. I am constantly surprised that people give up having company—such a beautiful word! No matter how simple my preparations, I love having company. It is one of the bests ways to keep from feeling old.

"But I get too tired," sighed a friend.

Maybe doing things elaborately is too much. But it I don't feel up to doing a lot of dishes or preparing a fancy meal, I buy pretty paper plates and plan a simple menu. It seems to me a matter of that old pride getting in my way if I insist on using my best dishes. After all, company is for conversation and sharing and doesn't depend on food at all. It is more exciting to feel in the stream of life than merely to conserve energy.

And I have found a most remarkable result. The more I yield to my wish to be *alive* and doing things, the better I feel.

I don't have to do it all with my own strength. Jesus will always loan me some of his if I ask. Life should not cease being an adventure, and it has not for me. I never know what idea a friend may suddenly offer to amuse or touch me. People never cease to be fascinating. No one can ever fully know another; it is seeking to know and understand all the complexities of a person that keeps me feeling alert and curious.

Friendship can even be found in a book or a letter or in my garden. In a very real sense, the whole universe is a friend because the beauty around me reminds me that my greatest and dearest friend is Christ.

Friendship is a form of love, and all love is eternal. It is difficult to lose lifelong friends, but that heartache too is part of life. The beauty of mutual caring is never lost, even though our friends have gone on ahead.

Chapter 4

Being Oneself

I remember many years ago trying to explain to my mother that I was *me* and didn't want to be like Susie or Mary or whoever the model of the moment was. I think this feeling of "me-ness" in small children is natural. And when we adults impose too much of *us* that creates a perversity in the child.

Certainly as we grow up, being one's own person is not always easy. I struggled for many years as a young person, never feeling at ease with myself. The challenge has carried over. It does not seem any easier in my so-called old age.

There is an answer. I have discovered that each of us is so unique it is a miracle.

Our uniqueness is very real. When I discovered that just adding up years really had little to do with how I feel inside, I threw out the idea that I had to fold up and meekly become resigned. God does not repeat patterns. The more I let go and let God manage my life, the more "me" I become. (This is not to say I don't have a lot of things in me which need correction.)

Being one's own self implies responsibility not only to grow, but to keep geniune respect for self and others.

As I observe other people in their 60's, 70's and up, it seems to me that those who are happy are genuinely mature. They are at ease with themselves. They do not accept that life is over as far as their importance is concerned. They accept difficulties and seek solutions.

I am myself. I can think I am an old woman, that my life is almost over—but I don't have to. I have a choice. I can feel that I now may live so that all the lessons I have learned, all the experiences I have lived, all the joys and sorrows and loves which have molded me give me a rich, *ageless* final time.

The last five years have been in many respects the most exciting and productive of my life. I think there is a depth of perception, intuition and compassion to be found in accepting life as it is *now*—a depth that escapes me if I worry about how old I am.

This new leisure opens up all sorts of possibilities. Anything I choose to do can be creative, if I just take one day at a time and plan to live it fully. Who ever knows what may happen? It can just as well be the happy unexpected as a disaster.

The senior centers offer all sorts of classes. It is possible to begin a new adventure in any subject which intrigues, whether political, cultural or purely creative. The world is full of things to do and my problem is to find the time and energy to do all the things I want.

One very mild and gentle friend joined a group which discusses current events, including politics. She finds herself enjoying arguments and controversy because it adds a bit of zest to her quiet life.

Another friend who held an executive position for years decided upon retirement to do volunteer work which would use the same skills. She became a coordinator of other volunteers in a hospital. She is quite happy—and is enriching her life and others'.

"Oh, but I can't do anything like that!" lamented a friend.

How does she know? I always thought the last thing in the world I could do was give talks or workshops. I have found I enjoy every minute of the sharing with others who are trying to meet the same problems.

One of the greatest joys in being old lies in finding new aspects hidden inside the person one thinks of as "me." My friend might discover she enjoys working now with children, or troubled teenagers, or less fortunate old people who are confined either at home or in a nursing home. Or maybe she could just be a listener and let troubled people talk to her. Giving love and compassion is a beautiful way of keeping in the stream of life.

Being one's own person brings spiritual and emotional maturity and all kinds of special rewards. One is the conviction that no one *needs* to become old. The body may and probably will; mine complains. But I have such a sense of wonder and oneness with the marvels of the universe that I feel *alive* and can only anticipate more delight in life.

Not that moments do not come when I feel let down, rejected, misunderstood. That is a part of life. It is not new. I remember feeling the same as a small girl, even more frequently in early adulthood as I faced the problems normal to that cycle.

It is not easy to feel enthusiastic when ill or conscious of depleted energy. That is time for self-discipline. And at times it really is just too hard. The spark of vitality burns too low.

Then I turn back, picking out the high points of my life and reliving them in memory. By the time I finish I find myself renewed and certain that life as a whole has been exciting and rewarding. And I see again that whenever I have had the courage to act on my own special inner uniqueness, I have felt whole.

Those times often came when I was experiencing a profound loss. When my husband died a few years ago, I was shattered. It took a long time to put myself together again. And then I found a new dimension to myself—a more profound capacity for love and compassion, a greater understanding of the meaning of life.

30

Everyone can remember painful times, but we did not draw away from life then because of the tears and anger of the moment. Why should we now? Instead of dreading old age, we can become more aware of our own uniqueness, built of all our adventures along the way. My way is like no one else's. My pain is different; my joy is not the same.

But creative power lies within each of us, and it need never grow dim or die. It is up to each of us to keep it alive—unless we want life to be drab. Let's stop being critical of ourselves and use these last years to do what we've always longed to do.

Believe it or not, my last spree was riding a merry-go-round—and not in a ladylike fashion sitting in one of the seats. No, indeed! I rode a horse that went up and down. And I enjoyed it immensely.

A friend suggested, gently, that *she* felt undignified doing such childish stunts. But I feel dignity is something quite different. The spirit within is eternal. I want to keep alive in me the sense of joy and fun children have (or should have).

Grandchildren are a special joy for this reason. My five-year-old thinks it is quite normal when I go running after him as he zooms around the yard. "Come on! Come on!" he shouts. (Life is a little like that. I feel it calling, "Come on!")

Quite possibly others may feel scandalized at the vision of an 88-year-old grandma dashing after a small boy. And it doesn't bother me at all to agree that is possibly not *their* way of being themselves. That is the joy of being unique, different one from the other. And just because we grow old, we do not have to stop running with life, whatever expression that may take. If something feels "right," then it is part of the "me" inside that sedate garment of age.

Running with my grandson is a legitimate expression of love for the little boy. Life is deepened and made more vivid when I become one with children because there is an eternal child in me. That is what imagination, enthusiasm and zest are all about. It was when I began to accept that God means for me to grow and mature in his love that I became free to be myself. I *am* a child—God's child.

It surprises me that so many old people seem to feel inadequate. Some are resentful, bitter because they feel put on life's shelf. It seems to me each of us is responsible for keeping the gift of life growing with each day.

Now is the time to live out the dreams that have been waiting for a lifetime. A friend of mine decided to rebuild an old piano. "What a lot of work!" some said. My friend did not think so. It challenged his mind and kept him excited and lively. And when it was finished, he felt an enormous satisfaction.

When I was about 80 I felt a need to get more deeply into life's creative stream. So I went back to writing, a lifelong love that had been pushed aside for more demanding matters for years. That is one reason I have no time to feel old. You cannot write without using your imagination, whether you are working with facts or fiction. It also creates a need for enthusiasm and discipline. It keeps me wondering what I am going to write next—and not for a minute do I expect to retire as long as I can write.

A creative interest need not be one of the arts. Another friend is hooking the most gorgeous rugs for her house. Part of the adventure of growing old is to delve into new creative activities.

It is not even important to discover I am not very good at a new effort. A few years ago it seemed wise to develop some sort of handwork for my coming old age (when I reach 100 or so). I began to knit a pair of socks. There was never a pair of socks like those! One got bigger and bigger and the other became smaller and smaller. Don't ask me why; I just developed a very original style of knitting. It provided considerable amusement to me and my friends.

Another friend decided to improve her cooking. Happily she invited a group for lunch and planned a really fancy dessert. It was to stand tall and proud in all its beauty. But when she took it out of the icebox, to her consternation it had collapsed in a heap. It too served as a source for laughter.

It isn't really necessary to be perfect. All that matters is to try what is appealing and never mind the raised eyebrows. Whatever form creativity takes, it is an expression of our uniqueness. Of all the periods of life, the older years are certainly the right time to use the freedom to be ourselves, the persons God wants us to be.

Chapter 5

Using the Senses

Few of us think about how much our senses add to our lives. Certainly I never gave it a thought until I began to hear people around me saying, "Now that we are all getting old..."

I didn't want to get old. I denied my years indignantly and vigorously. I had married later than usual and had my children later than others; sometimes I felt as if I was running behind time. Seldom did I remember that a lot of water had flowed under the bridge in a very interesting and varied life.

So I began to wonder how people keep from getting old—at least, from looking or feeling old. One of the things I learned from observation was to use my senses—sight, hearing, touch, smell and taste—to intensify life. Then there is no way to feel that life has turned gray and dull.

One day a few years ago I was up on Telegraph Hill in San Francisco. I lived there in my younger days when there were no high-rises, no Coit Tower. Goats then wandered around that attractive spot.

I remembered looking down upon the Embarcadero and seeing ships at anchor, looking off to the horizon and believing I could travel endlessly out there. I could hear again the chatter of Italian as black-eyed children raced up and down the steps of my apartment building.

Perhaps because the earlier memories were so sharp and clear, I began to think about the senses we have as I looked around me. I asked myself if I really look at things now and see them with the same imaginative sharpness.

That day I began an experiment. If I look at something—the sea, the mountains, art or people—I am no longer satisfied with a casual glance. I look for as much detail as I can see. How many colors can I see in the water? What shades or hues of blue? Last spring in Hawaii, looking out on the green slopes across from the hotel, I was able to count at least six different kinds of green.

Many of us think of eyesight mostly in connection with reading as we age. That is, of course, vitally important as our vision becomes less clear. I know from experience how trying reading becomes. But one of the great gifts which comes from trying to see everything in greater detail is that my thoughts and memory are filled with detailed scenes which may be a great comfort as my eyes grow dimmer.

Often as I read the New Testament, I am struck by the way Jesus noticed things around him. I think the great artists, too, are people who are profoundly aware of all the little things of life, things which so many of us never notice. Taking care really to see adds to the creative force in life, in each individual.

In my new consciousness of color, I have discovered that it really has a definite effect on my mood. It is fortunate that no one expects me to dress in the somber colors my grandmother wore, because I would rebel. I think that as I get older I will probably wear more and more gay colors. The dark colors belong to my youth, when I wanted to look sophisticated.

Why do so many old people wear drab outfits when it doesn't cost a cent more to have happy colors? No wonder a person feels "old" in dull, unexciting colors!

My vision is sharpened in another way as I learn to look beyond the superficial glance. The inner vision is stimulated in some way too. I no longer look at mannerisms or appearance in others, but for the little things that tell me about the real person. Some of this is called insight or intuition, perhaps, but partly it is a sharpening of the senses.

The same is true of hearing—or any of the senses. It is very exciting to let them have full play instead of being content with minimum use. Sharper hearing reveals the undertones or overtones in a person's voice. One might hear happiness or loneliness, anger at life or joy in growing older. A cry for help might go unheard if the ear is used only for surface conversation.

Even listening to city sounds is exciting. They are not just noises which irritate, but the sounds of life—and the imagination can translate them into the infinite variety of city life. The country has a completely different set of sounds, and all add to the color and rhythm of life itself.

Touch is a way of communicating. It is the expression of love, of tenderness, of comfort. Older people often need the touch of someone who cares. It is part of life, and there are already so many things with which we have had to part.

I do not think enough thought is given to how to use these gifts from a generous God. Certainly we, as older, mature people, need not fear using all our senses to give greater joy and richness to others.

One of the joys I have found in growing older is the freedom I feel to pour out love and appreciation. I no longer feel the shyness and self-consciousness I did when younger. Being more oneself enables a person to give more. I am convinced from my experiments with intensifying my senses that it not only adds to my life but enriches others as well. Being alive means using all the gifts God has given— giving all of self to life, to God. And how fully I live determines the value of my life to others. Those of us who have reached 70 or 80 should, I feel, be so full of the wonder of life that everyone else can catch some of the glow.

I think of an old friend who is crippled with arthritis and has few moments free from pain. One day we were talking about life and its meaning. "How do you feel about living confined to a wheelchair?" I asked.

She beamed at me, shook her head and leaned forward in her chair. "Honey, I am thanking the Lord for the gift of living."

"You don't mind getting old and crippled?"

"Oh yes, I mind. But the Lord doesn't want me yet. So I just keep on breathing and breathing until he fetches me. And I have eyes to see and ears to hear and a heart that loves."

She has nothing in common with another friend who constantly bemoans her increasing age: "I don't have any interest in the things I used to do."

That is all right. I find that many things once important to me no longer intrigue me. However, there are endless other things to do. And mind, imagination and awareness grow in finding them.

I do not believe that the zest for life has much to do with education or other "advantages." It is the spirit within and how we meet life's challenges that determine our old-age values. I am not speaking of those who meet real tragedy, such as mental deterioration—although I have known brave people who suffered profoundly in the knowledge that they were losing their capabilities and yet maintained courage to the end.

With each added year, I am more grateful that so much wealth is mine. I have to remember that

God is the source of all life, that mine is his gift. Perhaps we all need to recall the children's story about the little engine who kept saying, "I think I can, I think I can," and puffed his way up the mountain.

"But I have nothing to live for," sobbed a friend. "I don't see anything to be happy about in the world today. I hate not being able to do the things I have always done. And I dislike the way I am beginning to look—all those wrinkles and lines."

Another friend with a sense of humor answered her lament: "When I get up in the morning and see myself in the mirror I think the old girl doesn't look so bad. Then I put my glasses on and look again— and the effect is spoiled!"

A sense of humor keeps sharpening all our feelings and perceptions. A fairly recent stay in the hospital convinced me of my need for mine. My body decided to develop an arthritic spine, which turned me into a very stiff and pained old lady.

Because of the pain, I was given a sedative at bedtime. I heard nothing at all until a voice said, "Good morning, dear. I want to take your blood pressure."

"What time is it?" I asked groggily.

"A little after midnight," she answered cheerfully. "Now go back to sleep."

Almost before I got to sleep I heard, "Good morning, dear. I need your temperature."

"What time is it?"

"Three o'clock. Now go back to sleep."

Next time the "Good morning, dear" was a bit

groggy too. This time it was five o'clock and I lost a little more blood. "Leave me enough to go home on," I grunted.

"Sleep well now," the soothing voice replied, but I stayed awake, thinking about the vicissitudes of life. A hospital, I decided, is a wonderful place to find out about yourself but not a place to take yourself seriously.

There is no way I can live to be 100 and not have a few pains and wrinkles. However, I don't have to look discontented or glum. When all is said and done, beauty comes from within at any age, but much more so in the older years. Some of the most beautiful people I know are very old. And the light of Christ shines in their faces.

Chapter 6

Cycles of Time

The Bible tells us there is a time for everything, even for living to four score and 10:

> A time to be born, and a time to die;
> a time to plant, and a time to uproot the plant.
> A time to kill, and a time to heal;
> a time to tear down, and a time to build.
> A time to weep, and a time to laugh;
> a time to mourn, and a time to dance.
> A time to scatter stones, and a time to gather them;
> a time to embrace, and a time to be far from embraces.

A time to seek, and a time to lose;
   a time to keep, and a time to cast away.
A time to rend, and a time to sew;
   a time to be silent, and a time to speak.
A time to love, and a time to hate;
   a time of war, and a time of peace.

(Ecclesiastes 3:2-8)

The cycles in my life seem very clear. As a child I looked at life quite differently, as all of us do. I don't think I ever gave a thought to the idea that I would grow old. Adults were formidable, the ones who decided what I could do. If I desired to grow up at all, it was because I could then do what I pleased.

Each cycle of life has its own excitements and viewpoints. A child views the world with eyes that create to some extent what he or she wants to see. I remember telling my mother once that I was not "me" but a little girl the family had found in Paris.

Later my whole life was bound up in the vision of myself as a sort of magical Florence Nightingale doing all sorts of wonderful and beautiful things. By the time the cycle of young adulthood arrived, this had turned to a more practical approach.

One of the most exciting things about old age is to look upon life as a vast pageant, a tapestry of interwoven intrigue and variety which is being rolled out before me. Life is creating the plot and the scenery in many experiences. Some of the plot is my personal drama; part is that which I observe as I move along through the years.

Old age is a sort of mental and emotional diary

to be read at will. Those who are in their 70's and 80's have lived through many events which have colored their vision of life. For instance, that first great war, the war to end all wars, taught compassion to those of us who lived through all the partings and pains of those days.

Time is a mystery. I do not know about others, but I find myself at times living in the past as well as in the present. Perhaps because human nature does not seem to change much even though mores do, life is full of repetition. In our old age we contain all the history we have lived through.

Haunting moods sometimes touch me. A scent drifting down a lilac-lined street brings back a time long ago, and with it the emotions of that time. A song drifting in the air makes my heart pound, for it renews a feeling of pain that once filled me. I do not think I ever want to shrink away from the poignant feelings brought to life out of the past. I do not want to hold them too closely, of course, or I cannot go forward in life. However, they are part of me—my old age as well as my youth. They are what has made me what I now am.

There were cycles when pain shattered dreams and it seemed impossible ever again to be glad or happy. And yet when the pain had been overcome, there was a new strength. And now in the last years, when strength is needed, it is part of my inner being.

The cycle when college ended and I went off to the big adventure of meeting life on my own is part of my willingness now to move into another cycle, an era when I must give up rather than build.

Marriage and career are part of these present years. I remember with such beauty those first years, which seemed so difficult in the great depression of the 30's. And I can still see my firstborn, with spikes of black hair and wise blue eyes.

The triumphs and failures of the years leading up to this moment are drama. I can say, "I love life. I am reluctant to let go of any part of it. I am still seeking wholeness. Thank you, Lord, for the gift of being old."

Sometimes I have been fearful. Most of us have such moments. Would I be happy wherever I have to live if my strength wanes too much? Am I going to be able to get around, or will I be housebound? Am I going to lose my sight?

These problems have a way of creeping into my mind at times, and I have to start again to rouse the old indomitable spirit.

I don't think of love as something that was more vital in youth than it is today. I feel that as we age, love becomes deeper—love of nature, of friends and family, of life, of God. This is the abundant life the Lord promised. But perhaps today is one of those days in which I feel alone, separated from God and from my human family. I have to create within myself anew the feeling that God is holding out love to me, holding out his hand for me to grasp. Those days are poignant. I think it is best to face them and try to understand.

Sometimes I suddenly become conscious of time moving swiftly and I am not sure of my own ability to handle life. My energy is not enough. Or I may realize that death is not as far away as it was years ago. I am suddenly conscious of its approach and I rebel. I want to be with those I love. I want to do this or that and there is not time.

So I sit down quietly and open my hands to receive God's love. As I rest in quiet, peace comes to me. God is always with me, no matter what the situation. And I rejoice that for the moment I am living actively and fully. I accept life. And with it, in the end, I am willing to walk through the open door.

Being old is not always easy. I have moments of feeling it is too hard, it demands too much of me. When my eyes refuse to let me read I have to remind myself of all the wonderful gifts life has given me. A dear one in the hospital hurts the heart; it is hard to let a loved one go. I know the pain. But that is not just being old. All through life there are moments of giving up as well as moments of receiving.

Now is the time to share with a young person seeking the way through what seems a long and lonely road. How wonderful that because I have lived a long life, I can say, "It will not always be like this. Sometimes it is light, sometimes dark, but always keep moving toward the light."

One of the beautiful things I have found in my older years is the gift of silence. I don't know why we are so afraid of silence, why we feel so awkward and unsocial. Yet silence is one of the greatest comforts I have found. I get to know myself. I understand others in my silence. And I often feel the wonderful presence of Christ. I lose my fears sitting in the silence and thinking of God's love and how it has been with me all these years, guiding and sustaining.

Would I really want to be a person who has never known pain (if there is such a person)? No. I didn't like pain when enduring it, whether physical or emotional, but I realize that it helped me to grow. Without it, I would not be a living part of life. I would not be able to share the courage and beauty of others. I would be a robot. I try to remember that while feeling despondent at some of my elderly difficulties.

I think of one mother whose only son was lost in the desert with plane trouble. No one has ever known just how or why. This dear friend is a beautiful older person with no trace of self-pity, though I know the anguish she has endured. She has great compassion and outgoing love.

Just to know people who have grown old, who have risen above their suffering and are joyful people, is a reward. I think they are one of the gifts God gives me.

I believe our last years, whether long or short, should leave a legacy of courage, joy and love. These are as precious as the gifts great artists, painters and sculptors leave to posterity.

I know I will have problems as the years go on, and I may not have many years left. However, life is never without wonder to me. Imagination and a sense of excitement fill me with gratitude that I have been permitted to live so long. I feel very sure that whatever happens, God will take care of me.

I hope not to join the group of oldsters who

weep and wail because life is different. Of course it is—with every cycle it has been different. And I feel deeply for those who find nothing vital or wonderful in life now—whatever age they may be—because they are losing the excitement which never needs to end. A change in my environment will not change the beauty of nature or rob me of my wonderful memories. It will not take from me my imagination or my sense of beauty or even my friends.

It is quite possible, I am finding, to turn some of the most painful moments of life into the most beautiful if I hold to my faith and let God show me the way. It is in my pain that I learn to reach out to others and hold out my arms to those who are suffering with love and compassion.

For I know that all of us are on the same journey.

Chapter 7

Where Shall I Live?

One of the most painful problems of old age is having to give up a home. This is especially difficult for one who is alone. I know it will demand all the strength I possess. All the beloved things collected over the years, each with its tender and happy memories, must one day be parted with—at least, most of them. It will be like tearing the fabric of my life apart, even though I find it easier now to give up material things than I did a few years ago.

Often I think of my mother, who at 75 had to give up her home of many years. I remember with sadness how little I understood the pain she endured in parting from beautiful things collected over the years. I did not then realize how much suffering was bound up in that experience. I did not mean to be unsympathetic; I just had not lived long enough to listen from my inner ear for the undertones in her voice.

So I am not going to be hurt if my children do not understand my trauma should the day come when I have to move, for I realize that one of the wonderful things about aging is the growing capacity to feel with and for others. I will try to accept the fact that once again life is changing, beginning a new cycle and giving me an opportunity to grow.

If one has lived in a house for almost 50 years, it is not easy to make a decision to move out. I hope if I come to feel inwardly that it is necessary, I can do so with courage. Wherever I go will be new and strange and demand adjustments. I am training myself now to think of it as an adventure. My spirit is still young and stalwart enough to find happiness in a new home if I can see it that way.

Meanwhile, I am learning patience in many things—how not to be upset when the plumbing acts up on a holiday or the washing machine develops strange behavior which my husband could have corrected in five minutes. Against the day when it all becomes too much, I am taking the first steps in breaking away from my attachments, no matter how beautiful or beloved. I am giving things to my children and my friends, knowing they will find happy homes with them. I find joy in thinking dear people will share my love for my treasures.

A few months ago a friend some 10 years

younger than I said, "If I were your age and had your problems, I would live in a retirement home. Why don't you?"

Possibly I am just too lazy to go through the task of sorting out all my belongings and deciding what to take to a smaller place.

But as I thought about it, I decided that the real reason is that I do not yet have the deep inner guidance to make the move. I am, on the whole, happy with my life as it is. What I may eventually do, I am not sure. It is a decision I will face as old age makes readjustment necessary.

Meantime I observe my friends who have already made such a move. There are some lovely retirement homes, and my friends seem happy— quite glowing, at times, about how wonderful it is not to have to garden or cook.

But I think of the quietness of a place where there are no children, no pets. It would be like living in a hotel, no matter how charming. I am not old enough yet.

Someone else remarked, "You have children in other cities. Why not plan to move near them even if you feel you can't live with them?"

That thought has crossed my mind. I love my children and grandchildren, and they love me. However, I might easily create stress for them and for myself in such a move. Both families are very busy, with full schedules and many activities. And while I know some lovely people where they live, I would miss my old friends and all my activities. If I were unable to be active, what in the world would I do stuck somewhere where I did not know many people?

My children and grandchildren would be full of their own affairs. While I am sure they would give me what attention they could, inevitably I would spend many lonely hours. Maybe I would feel hurt and neglected. They would feel guilty and all of us would be unhappy.

I would like to stay in my own home as long as possible. It is far less expensive than the alternatives, and there are ways to manage fairly adequately. I might be able to have help a few hours daily if my energy declines, or have hot meals sent in. If I need greater assistance to remain at home, possibly a practical nurse could be hired for part of the day.

Of course there is the nursing home, but I have never been able to work up any enthusiasm for that way of living. I know there are nice nursing homes— in spite of the horror stories—places where only a few patients are accepted and geniune love and caring is offered. If I should reach the point where I am too helpless to manage at home, I would try to find such a place.

If ever I do move, I want to be fairly near my old home. I never want to be far away from the blue-gray bay of San Francisco. I love to ride the cable car up the city's hills. I want to stay near my own church and my old friends. (Since many of them are still in their 50's and 60's or even younger, I expect to keep them for a long time.)

I do not want a new environment and a new set of lessons to be learned. I know too many people who have moved far away from their homes only to find themselves homesick for old friends and familiar sights. And there are enough lessons to learn just trying to live joyously in the midst of problems.

Someone else suggested that it would be nice to have a companion come to live with me. Perhaps I sound very unsocial, but I can see difficulties in that situation. I have lived in this house almost 50 years; I have my own way of keeping it. I lived with a man I loved almost that long. The thought of having to adjust all my habits to those of another woman just as set in her ways seems to demand more adjustment than my energy permits.

Once when I talked in a workshop on aging successfully, one older man rather abruptly asked a question that amused me: "How do you feel about remarrying?"

My spontaneous reaction was, "At 87 I don't think I have much choice!" This brought a laugh, and another as I added, "Unless, of course, I marry a much younger man." But if I were a lot younger, say 20 years, I would marry again if the right man came along. I like being married.

Many older couples do marry—some in their 70's and 80's. If a person has kept flexible, alive and vibrant, I see no reason for not marrying. Love is not just for the young. Older people have learned so many lessons about life that if there is any congeniality of spirit the marriage is much less troubled by the problems the young face.

I do not see myself marrying anyone I had not known for some time. Neither could I marry without considering my children's feelings. But as I say, it is not a problem I need to worry about. I simply enjoy being in the company of men when the opportunity arises.

Really, I do not mind solitude. I have learned to live in it. When it is too much I go out or have company. I enjoy all my dear friends; I admire and love them. But the older I become, the more I feel a need for quiet and separation from others.

I have found that being alone and being lonely are two different matters. After my husband died, I knew many lonely feelings. As I worked through my pain and grief, I found myself drawing on inner resources. I began to find both spiritual and emotional satisfaction in learning to know myself and in thinking.

Of course, we have had to think all our lives. But as I relaxed into my solitude, I realized that I could begin to know God in a new way. I began to rely far more on his guidance deep within me, to listen for his voice directing my life.

In solitude I began to sort out many of my life experiences and to find out how they related not only to past time, but to now. At moments I felt genuine surprise at the thoughts which came from my deep self. This delight in solitude has nothing to do with refusing to reach out to others. Indeed, it has made me far more outgoing. Relationships are just as important in the older years as earlier, perhaps more so.

But I have decided that learning to live with myself—at any age, but particularly now in my late

80's—is vital. It is rather exciting to find that I really enjoy being myself! Perhaps others learn that faster; I was slow because I was always so critical of myself (and sometimes others). When I began to mellow and not be quite so severe with myself, I began to know the person I can become. I love that word *become*. It implies that no matter what my years may be, I am still growing.

To live with self happily and be able to meet the new demands of changing times both outwardly and inwardly, I just have to keep working at that person down inside the shell of my body. I find it is sound common sense to feel proud of whatever I accomplish in my new state of age. To withstand pressures, conflicts and pains, I find it necessary to work at remaining flexible—just as I have had to work at it all my life.

A tree sways in the wind; it may even bend until it seems as if it will break, then stands upright again. I must let myself bend with problems as the tree does in the storm. There is no way to escape the stresses of life at any age except to let go of the problem and give it to God.

I have had to become more adept at living in the now. Yesterday is gone forever, I am no longer living in it. I cannot live tomorrow. I can only live fully and completely in this moment, this hour, this day.

On awakening each morning I give thanks for another day. One hour a day is devoted to inspirational reading, the Bible or whatever seems vital to the moment. Then I am ready for my day, for whatever it may hold.

57

I try to plan at least one high point of pleasure each day, no matter how simple. It may be a phone call to someone who is an inspiration to me or a loving wish to help someone else to find joy in the day. If I wake up feeling old I promptly try to do something about it: music, a brisk walk, company. Feeling low is nothing new in life. It is just that nowadays when my energy is low I am sure I am falling apart.

But for this moment I am alive—and living in God's love. Whatever mistakes I may have made yesterday are gone, except for what I may have learned from them. I have this moment in which to offer love to the world in which I live, to be thankful for the many gifts which constantly flow into my life. And tomorrow is in God's hands.

Chapter 8

Avoiding the Traps

There are some very neat little traps just waiting to catch us in our later years. One of them is being critical with a capital C. I do not know why it is so easy to fall into this one. Perhaps it is a lack of self-esteem, or a subconscious desire to feel important because until very recently older people have received little attention. We weren't supposed to have ideas of our own anymore. We were just supposed to be nice old ladies or gallant old men.

That view makes me think of my maternal grandmother, a very pretty Southern lady who always pretended that my grandfather was the sole boss. She wore her black alpaca with its neat white collar and cuffs with style and was very ladylike. Whenever conflict arose, she promptly had "the vapors." All controversy instantly disappeared and a large bottle of something was administered while Grandma lay supine on the couch and the entire family tiptoed around.

The modern version of handling controversy is less delicate. I am always on guard when, in a group of older people, the conversation moves to declare the awful condition of the world or the outrageous state of morals or the ridiculously unattractive clothes young girls wear.

"The world has changed since I was a girl," someone is sure to remark.

Yes, it has. When I think of all the history that has happened within my own lifetime, it is exciting. I recall very well when the first telephone was put in my home, when oil lamps were discarded for gas and later electricity—not to speak of all the changes in welfare, social security and education. Not all the changes are an improvement over the times when I was a girl, but some of them are worth defending.

I am impressed by the difference in the way children are regarded. A child today is looked upon as a person, a unique individual—and in a wise family is treated as such. Children today develop because parents understand *their* needs rather than as parents decide is good for them. Today's young people would hoot at some of the restrictions young people of my day considered proper—perhaps wisely so.

Permissiveness may have gone too far, but it

certainly makes for greater independence and, if wisely guided, maturity of mind at a much earlier age. I find myself impressed by the thoughtful young people of today. I think there is a very real loss to both old and young when communication is shut off.

One grandmother I know grieves because she feels her grandchildren will not let her close to them emotionally. She loves them, yet she is constantly critical of their clothes, their manners, their ways of thought. Children and young people today will accept guidance only from the older person who tries to understand and wants to share points of view, not from one who harshly states that the young people are all wrong.

To be this kind of person requires flexibility of mind and emotions. Too many older people seem to assume that having lived a long life necessarily means having acquired greater wisdom than any other living people. This is a disastrous trap. Imagination is the source of better understanding.

Imagination is the mother of intuition, and I believe that oldsters should set the pace. Lack of this quick sense for the feelings of others creates loneliness. People who shine with a certain inner radiance are people with lively imaginations. They have kept themselves alive no matter what their age.

One way I have found to amuse myself while stretching my imagination is to go back in memory and try to put together a very different sort of life. Suppose I had chosen to do this instead of that; what might I have become? Or I pretend to be someone else, preferably someone I find baffling. I think the exercise adds to my ability to be compassionate and wise.

Being critical is especially damaging in relations with middle-aged children. The parent in us is strong. When a son or daughter is taking an unwise path in life, it is tempting to speak up. I have found that is an excellent way to alienate a child or grandchild.

Times *have* changed. The young people of today— even the middle-aged—live in a different era, a different atmosphere. I for one am trying to the best of my ability to add the mood of today to my years of growing experience. There is no way to feel genuine love and understanding with younger generations unless I am willing to open myself to what they feel and think. It is a privilege to share their lives.

I have such a deep feeling of reverence for the life God has given me; perhaps reverence for all life is the key to relationship with others. I do not ever want to lose the feeling of love for all with whom I come in contact because it fills me with a joy which has nothing to do with outer circumstances—health or money.

I have observed others caught in another very serious trap. I have been guilty of stepping into it myself: failure really to listen. Listening should be one of the finest arts of an older person. Too many of us talk too much. I am trying to discipline myself not to do so, but to listen with my heart as well as my mind.

Am I monopolizing the conversation? Is my subject of any interest to the others? I have sat in groups of older people where one person held forth until everyone was squirming. Yet the speaker does not seem to notice. Am I talking about myself in a self-centered way? Do I break into the conversation and start a whole new topic without regard to what has been said? One person I know makes me shudder. She relates her past on every occasion— and it is a boresome tale, at least as it is told.

Of course, these things can and do happen among younger people. Sad as it may be, I think it is more frequent among those in later years. Not listening is a trap we walk right into.

The art of listening is creative. We give of ourselves when we genuinely listen to what another is saying. People are wonderful, interesting and often contradictory—a source of endless enjoyment if we listen.

Too many older people have forgotten how to enjoy other people—or themselves. Why shouldn't we enjoy ourselves? While that includes activities and places to go, enjoying myself is much more than what I do. If I stop and think of all the things which have happened over the years I've lived, both in the world's history and mine, I feel important. It's not that I've accomplished anything important, but I am a cog in the wheel of life which constantly turns round and round.

I can enjoy places I've been. I remember the city of Bruges, Belgium, where I lived as a girl. I can still hear the sound of carts moving over cobblestones beneath my high dormer window, the quack of fowl on their way to market, the church bells ringing and someone whistling along the canal. This is part of my life. Remembering, I am renewed—young again.

Enjoying myself keeps me from falling into the trap of becoming indifferent to my appearance. Why should I stop caring what I look like just because I am old? I do not have a fortune to spend on clothes, but I can use good taste. I do not want garments which would look lovely on my grandchild, but neither do I feel that bright colors are too undignified for one of my years.

In fact, last year I succumbed to a beautiful bright red suit. The color vibrates around me joyously and I feel about 25 in it. I am a happier person when I wear colors that are bright and blithe rather than dull and gray.

The cultural myth that only the young are attractive is an illusion. Look at the faces of the elderly and see the beauty of life written on them: strength and courage, love and compassion. This is real beauty. It is time for us to think of ourselves proudly. We have lived!

Chapter 9

Stress and Compensation

Stress is not a new matter to the elderly. It is recognized as one of the major health problems at all ages. It is also recognized, however, that the older person may have to contend with greater stress. Problems become more serious. One begins to worry about where to live or whether health and income will hold up. Painful losses occur. People find themselves alone much more—sometimes the victims of real neglect.

Worse than the problems that develop is the fear of what tomorrow may bring. Many times I have wakened in the night and wondered how I am going to manage. I try to hold to the inspirational thought that I can begin anew with each new day, living now, this minute—but I cannot always keep this perspective. Too often I am reminded of the stresses rather than the compensations of age.

One of the reasons for our fear is the loss of self-confidence which seems to be part of growing old. Perhaps this is a product of the assumption that increased years have cost us our capacity to act, think and do. I think that too often we give up out of fear, not because of a real problem. Being old is a state of mind, not a matter of years.

A few months ago I had to spend a few days in the hospital. While there I wasted some valuable energy wondering if I could still take a long-planned trip to see some dear friends. I mustered up all sorts of old-lady arguments and almost succeeded in convincing myself I wasn't strong enough to travel— until my younger friends also began to hint that perhaps it would be wise to give up the idea.

My sense of adventure immediately popped back to life. Do stop talking old, thinking old, acting old, I promptly admonished myself. And I packed my suitcase and hopped (figuratively speaking) on the plane for Kansas. Not only did I have a delightful reunion with my friends, but the trip was a quick and easy cure for the "oh, dear, I'm so old" feeling. I came home feeling like myself again.

I think the hardest thing to face is the sense of confusion which sometimes comes in the early part of old age. It is not a new feeling; I remember as a child telling my mother that I didn't feel like "me."

Something similar happened to me in my 70's. I

did not feel any older as far as zest and enthusiasm for life was concerned (nor do I now), but many physical changes were taking place. Each decade seems to mean a new loss of energy—a fact I found hard to accept at that time. For a period I felt again as I did when I was a child. Who was this "me" who was suddenly clumsy and slow, who was not able to remember things as well? A sort of panic hit: Was I not going to have a clear mind?

I had to make adjustments in my thinking and feeling as well as in my activities. But once I accepted the changes as one more cycle in life, I found many new ways in which to enjoy myself. My fears may have a genuine basis, but I can find ways to overcome them.

. When the ability to remember names became a casualty, fear only made the problem worse. Worrying that I would forget the names of people I have known for years when there were introductions to make made me all tight inside—and their names were even harder to remember.

Fear is a negative emotion; it has no proper place in my thinking. Now I simply accept the fact that my memory is not as sharp as it once was. If I am caught in a moment of forgetfulness, I take refuge in avoidance. "This is one of my very good friends," I say, and smile most cordially while I go absentmindedly after the friend's name. Fifteen minutes later it comes to mind and I complete the introduction.

And of course I have found that my contemporaries suffer the same ailment. That discovery freed me to laugh instead of being upset.

I do make the concession of keeping careful daily notes of appointments. Important legal dates like the income or property tax deadlines are posted in a conspicious place. Sometimes I have to pin up notes to myself to remind me where I have put something. This is self-discipline and an admitted nuisance, but I should have developed the habit sooner. Five years ago I received a Christmas gift which I put away in a special place. I still wish I knew where that place is!

It is easy to become less clear about things when older. Having a routine conserves nervous energy and vitality. Flexibility is absolutely necessary, but the discipline of routine leaves more time for spontaneous action. I find it helps me to be creative.

Losing the quick memory of earlier years is not entirely amusing. I find this year it is sometimes more difficult to think of a word I need, and that is distressing. All of us dread mental deterioration. But it seems futile to worry about it. Keeping the mind active seems to be a better solution.

Not too long ago I took part in a delightful luncheon where most of the guests were in their 70's. This was a group of capable, well-educated people, but almost the entire conversation was about aches and pains, the dreadful state of the world today and the shocking attitudes of young people. I couldn't help but wonder why we let ourselves drift into these stress-related thoughts. Why let all the beauty of the world, the miracle of life with its love and joy be lost in negative feelings?

Life is a gift. I try never to forget that, no matter what happens. Again and again, as I ask myself if I am making the right response to life, I take all my problems into meditation and prayer. Unless I can build my years and my life on the rock that is God, I do not know how I can be a joyous person. It is not a matter of holding on to life as it was with grim determination. Rather it is a letting go in trust. God has been with me always; he will be with me now. I am still his child, living in his love and taking my last steps toward the Light.

If I feel out of the stream of life, it must be because I have permitted myself to get out of tune. There is no reason why getting older should create such a feeling. I have lived: suffered, rejoiced, made mistakes and done some things right. Surely I have something to pass on.

If I am alone more than I would like, frequently it is because I do not reach out and do the things I can do, or see the people I am free to see. The world is crying out for people to be interested in one another. I might visit a hospital or relieve a young mother who is overburdened and needs some time alone. I never need to be lonely if I am willing to give freely of myself.

I find that I can be as aware, as alive, as vibrant as ever. Indeed, one of the compensations I have found in old age is that many of the things which troubled me when I was younger are no longer problems. Instead of losing confidence, it seems to me, all of us should take pride in our long years and accumulated experiences and accept the stresses with serenity as one more cycle in life.

Another compensation I find is the ability to laugh where I would have wept when I was young. A sense of humor, which is sharpened and honed through life, gives a better perspective on what is important in life.

My wisdom, if I have any, has been built through pain as well as exciting experiences. I do not feel it necessary to give advice on every occasion, or even to express what I have learned. I still have much to learn. The fine art of living joyously will never be mastered. People are so complex, so wonderful in many ways, it will take all my days before I begin to understand.

Chapter 10

Facing Loss

Why does it seem so much harder to adjust to the pains of life now? Having less physical energy is probably one reason. Another is that I cannot keep as active as in earlier years; it is more difficult to put painful things out of mind.

I am quicker to grieve for others; their pain, too, is now mine. People seem so vulnerable. Though I have learned that compassion is one of the great lessons of life, often there is little I can do to give comfort.

I think of one older mother whose middle-aged daughter is paralyzed and in a coma after an automobile accident. There seems to be little hope of her recovery; yet that mother goes every day to visit her daughter. When she comes away, her cry is "Why? She had so much to offer and now she is no longer really alive." She is silent for a moment. "Why could it not have been I?" she asks.

I am sure any older person who sees a loved child hurt or a young person's life shattered feels as this mother does. I felt that way when a small grandchild was threatened by a crippling disease.

But I do not agree with the friend who remarked, "Who wants to be old? You fall apart physically; you have to give up so many things you want to do. You get sick or have something happen that takes all the joy out of life."

On the contrary, I find life richer because I am old. I have lived. I have seen the magnificence of giant redwoods, the color of sunsets over the sea. I have known the tenderness of holding in my arms a tiny baby, perfect in every way, and wondering at God's handiwork. I have heard great music, birds singing in the meadows and wind singing in the forest—and sensed the nearness of God. I have known love, the wonder of friendship, the comfort of a friend when I was in pain. Nothing can take my memories from me.

I no longer regret any of the hard things I faced in life or feel any bitterness. When I feel shattered, as I did when my husband died, I turn to the healing light of the Holy Spirit. The suffering I have endured has taught me compassion, empathy with others. A poignant acceptance of the universality of grief expands me—and whenever hands reach out to help, Christ becomes more real, more alive in this world.

I do not look upon the grief which may come to me now as another scar upon my heart. I know that I may grieve and overcome my grief; and that every experience—at any age—which makes me more conscious of love as Christ taught it enlarges my vision. It makes me a deeper old person who can rejoice and be glad that life has been lived so abundantly.

Often, perhaps, I forget that courage is a vital part of my life. Courage is not a quality of youth, but an eternal quality which I accept as a gift from God. The courage I mean is the profound belief that everything that happens in my life is in some way meant to help me grow.

Too long the attitude toward the elderly has held that at a certain period people must retire from life. I am grateful that such a viewpoint is finally being denied. I do not for a minute believe that I am supposed to stop being a growing, vibrant person as long as I am alive. I expect to continue to change as long as I have the breath of life. I anticipate that each day has something of beauty in it and perhaps something of grief. As long as I cope, feeling that I am in the stream of life, I am not afraid.

Some of the minor griefs that come to anyone with age are a little deafness, a dimming of vision, a growing inability to get around easily. Many young people have to meet these same problems and face them for a lifetime. So it should not be too difficult for me, having lived many years without handicaps. I think part of staying eternally youthful lies in how these problems are met. I hope I face them with an indomitable spirit.

The first thing I have to do is accept the fact that it is not a calamity if I do not hear as clearly as I did. I am not deaf enough to feel the sense of isolation which many people suffer. I feel a deep compassion for those who do.

I know one older woman, very dear to me, who has always been a very self-sufficient and successful person. She has lost all hearing. But she has not lost her feeling for life and for other people. She does not permit her pride to make her withdraw from painful social situations. She goes out; she invites people in. She uses a pencil and pad to communicate without any show of embarrassment. If she feels isolated, it does not show. Her manner is warm and outgoing and she always manages to make those with her feel comfortable and pleasant.

To me, she wears the badge of courage in a very inspirational way.

The problem of dimming vision is more difficult for me to accept. All my life I have been an ardent reader. I have always loved and responded to the beauty of nature. I have always had excellent sight, and I am finding it not altogether easy to face the fact that I am now very limited. The vision in one eye is gone; I can only distinguish light and dark. The other eye is still good, though. I find it important to give thanks constantly for that much vision.

My failing sight means I must make some changes in my life which I do not find easy. I am learning patience because it is much harder to carry out daily duties, even little things like noticing if there is dust around. I must try to find other worthwhile activities which come within my physical scope. I believe some door will open for me in a way I do not yet know.

The big thing I am learning is a greater understanding of those who cannot see at all. I am so very fortunate because I carry in my mind all the lovely things I have seen, all the places I have been, all the dear faces. And I can still read enough to help me through the day. If the other eye gives out too, then I will have stored up many memories to carry into the new world I will have to enter.

I know as I get older I will have to face more of the physical problems which are part of aging. If I worry too much about it, I will just aggravate the problem and upset others. One thing which helps me accept what I must is not to let anything make me forget that I have an abundance of living behind me; I need not feel inferior now. I am still a beloved child of God.

No one says that the problems of aging are easy to face. None of them are. All of us probably shed tears when we first realize that our daily way of living is changing in ways we would not have chosen. But life is still a gift, and like many another gift, it becomes more valuable with the passage of time.

I do not believe God will mind if I feel upset when handicaps enter my life. My relationship with him is the only answer to many of the problems which arise. I have searched for the belief that he is

81

directing my life, and I have found it increasing in the last few years. I am sure that whatever happens, God will be with me.

God has enriched my life so greatly up to this moment that I am not afraid of the next steps. I have known illness, pain, suffering, loss—and always I have felt the everlasting arms beneath me. I try to be obedient, to listen in deep silence for God's plan for me. But for a person long independent it is not easy to say, "Take my life and let it express the Christ in every thought, word and deed," and mean it.

Grief touches me when I first begin to feel this part of my life, or that, become difficult. Then the inner voice tells me, "The core of you is eternal. So give yourself fully and completely to this cycle of life. Sit back and enjoy it. Feel love pour through your grief and change it to joy."

It can be done. Not alone, but in accepting the love God pours out on the world, the love which comes to me through the beauty around me and from my family and friends.

Grief can be the means of growing spiritually if it is accepted with grace. To grow is the purpose of life, surely, to search for the meaning in all the things which happen to us.

Old age is a culminating experience, a summing up of all my personal history. Dignity and integrity are part of aging, which means that I am gaining something in spite of what I lose.

No one, of course, ever knows how long his or her time on earth is. But once we reach a 70th birthday, we begin sometimes to wonder about death. That is not a morbid thought, but a very natural one.

I do not dwell on the thought of death, but I do think about it. I do not fear death. Like most older people, I pray that I will be spared a long, drawn-out and painful illness.

For now, I live each day fully and completely. I awaken each morning with thanks for the new day and all that it may mean. I try to walk as serenely as possible in the light which Christ offers me, assured that I am not alone but supported by his love. I try not to let any opportunity to express joy and love and appreciation slip by.

I am sure of my eternity. I am sure that just as I have gone through many cycles in my lifetime, I can find peace and serenity in the acceptance of death when it comes. I think people who worry about it are already letting themselves die a little. I have been given the gift of life; I am sure it is eternal. Someday I will walk through that open door into another world. I am not afraid.